The Care and Feeding of

Stuffed Animals

By Glen Knape
The Care and Feeding of

Stuffed Animals

Photographs by Jeanne Hamilton

Harry N. Abrams, Inc., Publishers, New York

Preface

Any book as unusual as this is bound to cause a certain amount of controversy. Many readers will wonder if I'm serious and if the book is true. Well, I am and it is. *The Care and Feeding of Stuffed Animals* is based on years of experience, study, and conversation with a great many stuffed animals. While readers who have little experience with or empathy for stuffed animals may be unable to accept this, those who own and communicate directly with stuffed animals will be able to confirm it.

The Care and Feeding was written for the great majority of people who know and love stuffed animals but cannot communicate with them. It is our hope that the information provided here will enable owners to give their friends the love, care, and affection that all stuffed animals need.

Introduction

Stuffed animals are rapidly becoming the world's most popular pet. Since they need little space and offer a wider variety of shapes, sizes, and traits than any other animal, this is not at all surprising.

Because of their modest needs, it is as easy to have a family, or "huggle," of stuffed animals as it is just to have one.

Almost invariably friendly, they seldom if ever bite.

They offer both the amateur and professional breeder a delightful challenge.

When kept clean, stuffies are odorless and, if properly cared for, will remain healthy and active for many years.

Unfortunately, their lives are frequently interrupted by accident or neglect. This is caused by a serious lack of information. No source of instruction on the proper care, feeding, and safety of stuffed animals exists. Without these vital facts, many well-meaning owners have unwittingly neglected or injured their stuffies. We hope to remedy this situation by informing stuffie owners of the needs of their pets.

But there are limits to the usefulness of a small manual. The variety of needs, tastes, and goals of stuffed animals cannot be covered in this small space. This manual is a good source of general advice but should not be used as a final authority. The final decision must always be left to the stuffed animal and his owner.

Dedicated to Stuffies Everywhere

Editor: Phyllis Freeman
Designer: Darilyn Lowe

Library of Congress Cataloging in Publication Data
Knape, Glen.
   The care and feeding of stuffed animals.

   Summary: Traces the history of stuffed animals from
prehistoric times to the present; provides guidelines for
buying and adopting them; and advises the new owner
on the care, training, breeding, and showing of stuffies.
   1. Soft toys—Anecdotes, facetiae, satire, etc.
[1. Soft toys—Wit and humor. 2. Toys—Wit and humor]
I. Hamilton, Jeanne, ill. II. Title.
PN6231.T673K6   1983   394′.3   83-7288
ISBN 0-8109-0789-5

© 1983 Harry N. Abrams, Inc.

Published in 1983 by Harry N. Abrams, Incorporated, New York
All rights reserved. No part of the contents of this book may be
reproduced without the written permission of the publishers

Printed and bound in the United States of America

Contents

1. History

The evolution of stuffed animals is very difficult to trace. The absence of a skeletal structure prevented fossilization. Their "borrowed" fur and stuffing make identification uncertain. And the disinterest of archaeologists has resulted in an appalling lack of serious investigation.

While much information has nevertheless been gleaned by a handful of dedicated researchers, stuffie history is not clearly documented until 1902, when the first "teddy bear" was born. Debate still rages in scientific circles over the nature and cause of stuffed animal development prior to that date. While the following evolutionary history is the best that can be offered at this time, it is somewhat speculative and far from complete. Much work remains to be done before stuffiology can attain serious recognition from the scientific community.

Totemic Period

The first stuffed animals were spiritual intermediaries. Paleolithic man wanted luck and safety in hunting. Using fur, bone, sinew, and other natural materials, he constructed a likeness or totem of his predators and prey. These totems were the centers of ceremonies designed to influence the actions of various animals. Remains of these totems, found in caves in Europe and the Middle East, have been dated at over forty thousand years.

The most common example was

In this ingenious scientific reconstruction, cave dwelling animals are seen in their natural habitat.

Left: Modern stuffiologists theorize that these remains of stuffed animal totems are over forty thousand years old.

One of the last furred stuffies, this specimen was found in a remarkable state of preservation in the corner of a cave.

the Cave Bear Totem. The so-called Cave Bear Cult was very widespread, suggesting that if any stuffed animals were to survive, the bear would be the most likely.

Some researchers believe that this was the case. If so, today's teddy bears may be direct descendants of the ancient stuffed cave bear. But this is only speculation, for there are no examples of linking species.

Intermediate Period

Stuffed animals were almost wiped out by agriculture. As the importance of hunting waned, so did the need for stuffed totems. The Cave Bear Cult gradually died out, and stuffed totems were no longer produced.

In addition, furred animals were becoming scarce. Little of this precious material could be spared for unessential purposes. Stuffed animals were perilously close to extinction.

Man's ingenuity came to the rescue at the last minute. This fortunate eventuality was due to several events.

Children have always imitated adults. This was as true in paleolithic times as it is today. Men performing serious rituals were mimicked by their young children. The large totems had their smaller copies.

When the totems died out, the toys lived on. While the species was threatened for a time by the scarcity of fur, the domestication of wool-bearing

animals and the invention of the loom provided other materials to secure their future.

Unfortunately, no examples of Intermediate stuffed animals have survived. The movement out of caves into more fragile man-made structures prevented the preservation of archaeological evidence. The ruins of a hut are much less protective of stuffie remains than the dry corner of a stone cave.

Toymaker Period

The Modern or Toymaker period began in 1902 when Morris Michtom made a stuffed bear symbolizing President Teddy Roosevelt's refusal to shoot a captive bear. Mr. Roosevelt gladly gave permission for the use of his name, and the first "teddy bear" was born. Few sold at first, but by 1906 they were selling quite briskly. With this popularity and vast increase in numbers came a natural diversification of the species.

Breeders found the creation of new varieties both simple and profitable. New materials were tried and new forms produced. These new materials, forms, and varieties have so enhanced stuffie popularity that most of today's children have at least one.

Stuffies should be taught about President Teddy Roosevelt's generous action to save their forebear.

2. Choosing Your Stuffed Animal

Where to Buy

Both human and animal psychology recognize the influence of early experiences on later growth and development. Stuffed animals have several such experiences before they are adopted. When the prospective owner recognizes and understands these influences, he has a much better chance of finding the stuffie he wants.

Unfortunately, formal studies of stuffie psychology are scarce and inconclusive. We have to rely on informal interviews of stufflings (baby or child stuffies) for much of our understanding of early stuffie life. These interviews reveal seven types of breeding and adoption agencies, each of which has its own effects on the growth and development of stuffed animals.

The breeders make the first and most important impression. Not only do they design and build the bodies that stuffies live in, they are also responsible for the stuffling's very first impressions. These are critical factors in a stuffie's growth and development. When the shopper knows which type of breeder bred a stuffling, he can have a good idea of that stuffling's potential.

1. Factory Breeders: This type has both positive and negative effects. The environment of a large factory does not provide the social contact necessary to healthy emotional growth and development. Assembly line

Left: The negative aspects of store environments are not surprising. Being displayed like a ripe tomato would damage anyone's ego.

workers must maintain their pace regardless of the problem a particular stuffling may be encountering with his newly attached arm or foot. Usually, the damage is minor, impermanent, and easily corrected by a loving owner (see chapter 3).

Many of the breeders who own and run factories are genuinely concerned about the stuffies they produce. Their work to increase the quality and appeal of their stufflings has been very beneficial. The most deserving breeders are recognized with the Teddy Roosevelt Best Breeder award, which is presented annually by STUFF (see Glossary).

2. Profit Breeders: This group does not deserve praise. They breed stuffed animals solely for profit, use cheap materials and poor designs, and handle their stuffies with indifference. The materials include stuffing that shrinks or crumbles and fur that is sparse and loosely anchored. The designs are bad imitations of those popular thirty years ago. The treatment they receive is completely lacking in personal contact. Their limbs, body, and facial features are stamped out by huge machines, and sewn together and crammed with stuffing by hurried workers.

These practices produce stuffies that are permanently damaged. No amount of love and attention can completely heal the wounds of this malicious behavior. It can only be

hoped that popular outrage will eventually force them out of the breeding business.

Fortunately, these extremists have their mirror opposite:

3. Artisan Breeders: There are still a few of these producing through a cottage industry. By working at home, among children and mature stuffies, they offer the most wholesome environment possible because the artisan understands and enjoys stuffies. His mature stuffies have counseled thousands of young stufflings, and his children know how to care for stuffed animals. Stufflings bred by them have confidence and insight that cannot be obtained anywhere else.

Adoption agencies are next in importance to breeders. By their actions they mold the self-esteem of the stufflings in their care. Since the style of each of the agencies differs, their effects differ also.

4. Department and Toy Stores: Some of these have been accused of producing negative effects. Being displayed like ripe tomatoes would injure anyone's ego, and stufflings are very impressionable. But this does not mean that all these stores are entirely negative. Their convenience and price have made stuffies available to people who could not otherwise afford them. And the comradeship that develops among stufflings who attend the same camp (as they often refer to their tem-

Store living fosters close ties among bunkmates, and annual
reunions are a high point of their year.

porary home) may endure for a life-time. In fact, reunions among former bunkmates are a high point of their year.

5. Craft Stores sell stufflings made by artisan breeders. These stores often share the love and affection for stuffed animals felt by owners and artisans. So they take special care to see that each stuffie receives the attention he needs. Often they keep experienced stuffies on hand to reassure new stufflings. Naturally stufflings found in this environment will be healthy and happy. They make excellent companions for adults and children alike.

Other agencies sell stuffies who have been or are being abandoned by their owners:

6. Thrift Stores: Usually operated by a charity on a nonprofit basis, they have no time for healing physically damaged and emotionally distressed stuffies. These are frequently discarded or sold as they are. This is one of the worst fates that can befall a stuffie.

But there is another that is even worse:

7. Garage or Yard Sales: Selling a stuffie in this way demonstrates a total disregard for the feelings of the stuffie. It produces an emotional devastation that is unparalleled. An owner that does this to one stuffie may be unable to regain the trust of any stuffed animal.

Signs of Good Health

Since few veterinarians have studied stuffed animals, and other professional help is almost impossible to find, it is extremely important that your stuffies be healthy from the start. But without information on stuffie health and disease, few owners know what to look for. A simple gauge or test is needed.

However, modern stuffies vary considerably, and many breeds have little in common. This makes a universal test difficult to design. Fortunately, several common features can still be discerned. These include stuffing, fur, limbs, and facial details like nose, ears, and eyes. These features should be carefully examined when checking for sloppy breeding practices, or damage from negligent or excessive handling.

The standard test is simple, takes only a few seconds, and can prevent much pain and anxiety:

Fur should be abundant, silky, and firmly rooted to the skin. Avoid stiff plastic-looking imitations.

Stuffing should be firm, yielding, and resilient. A granular or crunchy stuffing often degrades or settles, causing flopsy (see Glossary).

Thread placement and skin strength control seam quality. Close-spaced stitches in a tight weave are best. Beware poor construction and cheap materials. These can lead to seam rip and other disorders. And

Fur should be abundant, silky, and securely rooted to the skin.

Left: The ears, eyes and nose can be problem areas. All of them must be firmly sewn on (not glued).

When stuffie and shopper harmonize, recognition takes place, and the stuffling is purchased and taken home.

while nylon thread is sufficiently strong, it tends to unravel under frequent handling.

The legs, eyes, ears, nose, tongue, and tail can also be problem areas. All of them must be firmly sewn on (not glued). The eyes should be bright and expressive. Arms and legs must be sturdy enough to support the animal through many adventures.

These tests are an essential aid to choosing healthy stufflings who will lead long joyful lives.

How Stuffed Animals Help You Choose

All stufflings look forward to adoption. It is one of the high points of their lives. They discuss it longingly among themselves and anxiously examine every shopper who passes by. But they don't just observe. They participate in the choice.

When stufflings sense the approach of a shopper, they straighten their fur, put on their biggest smile, assume their cutest pose, and radiate their quality or expression of love.

If a shopper is open and receptive, he will sense that quality, and if they harmonize, recognition (see Glossary) takes place, and he purchases the stuffling.

A healthy specimen—note the bright, expressive eyes.

Older Stuffed Animals

Many owners adopt their first stuffed animal without having any understanding of stuffie needs and abilities. They have no more idea of how to care for a young stuffling than the stuffling has of life in a house. Both novice owner and young stuffling need the help and advice that only a mature stuffie can provide.

A mature stuffie will introduce his novice owner to the fine art of stuffie care, and advise and educate the stufflings in his "huggle" (gathering of stuffed animals). Every huggle should have at least one older stuffie. Their unique wisdom just can't be found anywhere else.

Unfortunately, it takes many years to raise an older stuffie, and since few adoption agencies appreciate their value, they're very difficult to find. Unless the novice is given one by a friend or relative, he must frequently resort to garage sales and thrift stores.

The First Night Home

While stufflings look forward to their new life, they do miss their old friends. Most have never been in a home before, and are a little nervous in the strange environment. If left un-treated, this nervousness can develop into "homesickness," a potentially seri-ous illness. Its symptoms are easily spotted (wanting to hide or to go home, refusing to play) and will disap-pear immediately if proper steps are taken.

3. The New Pet

Like an older brother, a mature stuffie can give a young stuffling with a novice owner the reassurance he needs.

Left: When an owner spots the onset of "homesickness," a potentially serious illness, he should form a "huggle." Then leave the stuffies alone so they can talk in private.

Every stuffed animal needs a spot of his own. Academic types inhabit library shelves.

If the owner has other stuffies, he should form a huggle as soon as possible. Place all the stuffies (including the new stuffling) in a circle (facing in so everyone can see everyone else) on a soft level surface (a bed is perfect) and introduce everyone to the new stuffling. Then leave them alone so they can talk in private. The older stuffies will explain what it is like to live in a house, and will help the stuffling feel at home.

Don't worry about interrupting the huggle when you return. Stuffies are very sensitive to their owner's presence, and always know where you are.

Your Stuffed Animal's Spot

Every stuffed animal needs a spot of his own. Its location is chosen on the basis of the needs and tastes of the stuffie and his owner.

Taste differs from one stuffie to another. Some like to see and be seen (from atop a dresser, for instance), and others like to hide behind lamps or under tables. Academic owls inhabit library shelves; monkeys and other athletic types hang out in lamps, backpacks, and bicycle baskets; and many bears like to hibernate in closets, desks, or dark corners. Most stufflings have never had a spot before, and will be unsure of themselves at first.

Be patient, and help them try several likely locations. After a month or two, they will settle down and spend most of their time in one spot.

Some stuffed animals are particularly curious, and like to wander about the house. These wanderers usually choose at least one spot in each room they frequent.

If you find that one of your stuffies is a wanderer, then be sure to pay close attention to the "Environmental Safety" section of chapter 5.

Disciplining Your Stuffed Animal

Not all stuffed animals are perfect. Some occasionally misbehave, and must be corrected. But the method can be difficult. Spanking is a futile exercise—rather like beating a pillow. They don't eat dinner, so it can't be taken away from them. And they live in their room, so sending them there won't work either.

These disciplinary measures were designed to correct physical behavior. But stuffed animals have very little physical behavior to correct.

Actually, the proper discipline technique is simple. Tell the stuffies that the behavior in question is not acceptable. Imagine the correct activity, and gently but graphically tell them how to behave. The exact phrasing will depend on the maturity of the stuffies and the behavior in question.

Be firm, but gentle, and insist on correct behavior. A good hug is always a nice ending.

A semihibernating panda makes this spot his own.

What to Feed

One of the many difficulties that arise from the neglect of stuffed animals is the ignorance of basic dietary needs. Although there is a mountain of information on the nutritional needs of dogs, cats, horses, cattle, pigs, and poultry, no study of stuffed animal diets has ever been made.

The information we do have is very sketchy, and by no means complete. It is presented as a tentative guideline only, and should not be considered final. We just do not have enough information for advice in this area.

The chief factor affecting stuffie nutrition is the stuffie's lack of internal organs. As a result, their requirements for physical food are very low. Many have been known to go for decades without a single bite to eat. But since their primary activity is emotional, they have substantial emotional needs. Their nutritional needs are thus emotional in nature.

They have words for a multitude of emotional types and qualities, just as we name and experience everything from horseradish to broccoli. Each of these qualities has its own effects, and meets a specific need.

Types of Food

Stuffed animals are not picky eaters. They'll take food in any form. There's little food value in jewelry,

4. Feeding Your Stuffed Animal

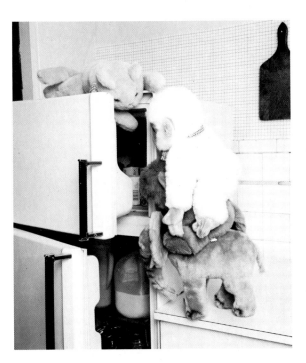

While every stuffie needs a portion of the major food groups, their individual requirements vary.

Left: Even if the cups are empty, stuffies like to have tea parties.

cars, fur coats, or other "things." But because many new owners are unaccustomed to expressing or receiving love without an easily identifiable package, we will mention some of the more popular forms:

    1. Hugs: A great favorite, especially among stufflings.

    2. Huggles: The all-around No. 1 big happy.

    3. Flowers: Stuffies enjoy flowers very much, especially when still attached to the plant.

    4. Clothes: All stuffies like to

Stuffies enjoy flowers very much, especially when still attached to the plant.

Although many stuffies have been known to go for decades without a single bite to eat, they do need to get out once in a while. Let them *experience* the great outdoors.

dress for plays, concerts, parties, and shows, particularly in outlandish costumes.

5. Outings: Stuffies like to go places. Picnics, hikes, bike rides, and visits to friends are much enjoyed.

6. Parties and Shows: Offer all the above and more.

This is of course only a sample. The possibilities are endless.

Nutrition

If a stuffed animal is to remain healthy and happy, he must be given a wholesome mix of each of the major food groups. These include games, outside events, quiet times, and learning experiences.

1. Games: Stuffies need to play. It stimulates their interest in the world and keeps them alert and active. Games like hide and seek, blindman's buff, and leapfrog are old favorites, and stuffies really enjoy a gentle tussle with their owner.

2. Outside Events: While stuffies are very sensitive to sunshine, rain, wind, and other outdoor hazards, they do need to get out once in a while. Take them for a walk in the park, a stroll on the beach, sailing, hiking, jogging, or on any activity that lets them experience the pleasant side of the great outdoors.

3. Quiet Times: Peace and quiet is every bit as necessary as play. The best quiet times are spent in the owner's company watching a fire in

Stuffies like to go places.

the fireplace, reading a fun book, taking a nap, basking in the sun, or anything that lets you be together.

4. Learning Experiences: Stuffies have a strong sense of wonder that should be fed from time to time. Watch an educational TV program with your stuffie, read a science book together, take him to the local science museum, or do anything that teaches the stuffie something about the world outside your home.

While every stuffie needs a portion of each of the major food groups, their individual needs vary. The precise needs of every stuffie must be determined by the stuffie and administered by his owner. While this may sound complex, it is really quite simple. Just love. That's all any stuffie really needs.

Supplements

Well-fed animals seldom need supplements. But it is nice to give them a little extraspecial treat. Treats add variety to their lives, prevent boredom, and help them look forward to your time together.

Treats add variety to a stuffie's life and prevent boredom.

Environmental Safety

Stuffed animals are very curious, and often wander about when no one is looking. They like to peek in nooks and crannies, and have been known to slip and hurt themselves, or become trapped in a dangerous spot. For safety's sake, we recommend the following precautions:

1. Give every stuffie a tour of your home. Point out the dangerous objects and situations. Explain doors, drawers, wall sockets, and light switches. Make sure your stuffies know what is and what is not safe!

2. Keep the doors to major appliances (ovens, washers, dryers, refrigerators, etc.) closed at all times.

3. Garage, laundry, and bathroom doors should remain shut. Especially at night.

4. All standing water (in sink, toilet bowl, bathtub, etc.) should be covered or drained. If you have miniature stuffies, be sure that the garbage disposal is covered.

5. The fireplace must have a sturdy screen.

6. Other pets should be kept away (even gentle play with a dog or cat can seriously injure a stuffie).

If a stuffie is being careless despite reasonable precautions, then the discipline procedure outlined in chapter 3 will quickly correct him.

While it would be simpler to keep your stuffies shut up in your bedroom, this would be a cruel restriction that could lead to frantic (and much more

5. Stuffed Animal Environment

Left: Give every stuffie a tour of your home. Point out the dangerous objects and situations.

dangerous) activity when they finally do get out.

Environmental Variety

Stuffed animals often suffer from cabin fever. This usually results from their owner's habit of closing the door to their room. Even the most active stuffie is unable to open a door by himself. He lacks the necessary strength and reach.

Like all higher animals, stuffies need variety if they are to remain alert and active. When constantly confined, they are denied this variety. While leaving their door open when you are away will help, it is only a partial solution. Once in a while they will want to "get out of the house." They won't always tell you this. Sometimes you will have to figure it out. But you will learn the signs. A sudden request that you rearrange the furniture is a good indication.

There are all kinds of things you can do when this happens. Take them shopping, to a movie, for a walk, on a picnic, to visit a friend, anything. But take them out and have a good time. It's much easier than moving furniture.

Environmental Quality

Stuffed animals have very clean habits. They never soil or litter their spot, preferring that it be kept clean at all times. This is also true of the house in which they live. They dislike getting

Stuffed animals are very curious and often wander about when no one is looking.
They like to peek into nooks and crannies, and have been known
to become trapped in dangerous spots.

Like all higher animals, stuffies need
variety if they are to remain alert and active.

mussed during their explorations, and
will occasionally leave a cobweb
draped over an ear or nose to show
that it is time something was done.

Since stuffies do not get to bathe
very often, there are some things they
carefully avoid. These include kitchen
garbage, cigarettes, fireplaces, fur-
naces, attics, and oily garage floors.
These have an odor or residue which
stuffies do not want on their bodies.

If a stuffie is being careless despite reasonable precautions, use the discipline procedure outlined in chapter 3.

Below: Once in a while, they will want to get out of the house. They won't always tell you this.

Most are easily avoided, but cigarette smoke is not. Stuffies will appreciate help in avoiding this odor. Simply move them, or ask your guests to smoke elsewhere.

There are several other items that should be mentioned.

Stuffed animals are very sensitive to alcohol. This is because their stuffing absorbs all of it. While most of the liquid will evaporate, the toxic chemicals remain behind. These chemicals have so strong an effect that most stuffies are rendered incoherent. In that case, the only cure is a thorough soaking in clean water. This in itself is a dangerous enterprise. Consequently, it is advisable to put stuffies out of harm's way when giving cocktail parties.

Stuffed animals usually have a musical preference. But since this is learned from their owner, there is seldom any conflict. The same is true of the visual arts, but stuffies' taste in room furnishings is often affected by their spot preferences.

That covers most of the pertinent areas. In general, when unsure of your stuffies' needs, ask.

6. Handling and Grooming

Thousands of stuffed animals are needlessly injured every year. A few of these injuries are caused by careless or uncaring owners, but most are the result of owner ignorance, and could easily be avoided. All their owners need is a little training in proper handling procedures.

Unfortunately, the proper procedure can be difficult to determine. Stuffies are individuals with individual needs and tastes. Every owner has to learn the needs of his particular pet. And the learning process can be very frustrating. Especially if the owner is unaware of his stuffie's instructions.

With other animals these directions are obvious. A puppy yelps, a kitten cries, and a piglet squeals. But stufflings don't "say" anything. They don't have the vocal capacities of other animals, and communicate by other means. The owner has to know either the proper way to handle them, or how to listen to the signs the stufflings give. This can be very difficult.

Proper Handling

We would like to describe "the" proper way to handle stuffed animals, but we can't. There isn't "one." The incredible variety of stuffed animals demands an equal variety of handling methods. You can't handle a giant like a miniature, or a bird like a bear. They each have their own needs.

Fortunately, there are several guidelines to direct owners toward the proper method for each stuffie:

Left: Stuffies have individual needs and tastes, which every owner has to learn.

1. Always pick up and hold a stuffie just as you would any animal of the same size and shape (i.e., dog, bear, hamster, elephant, etc.).

2. *Never* lift or carry a stuffie by his ears, legs, tail, head, arms, or nose. The constant strain can weaken even the sturdiest seam—and it puts the stuffie in a very undignified position.

These guidelines are introductory in nature and limited in scope. In making them broad enough to cover all stuffed animals, the details required for individual care are lost. These details have to be learned directly from the stuffie. If his directions are carefully followed, then most injuries will be avoided.

Grooming

Stuffies are very tidy animals, and like to be kept neat and clean at all times. But frequent handling, and the environmental hazards mentioned in chapter 5, inevitably muss their hair and attract dust and dirt. This may necessitate a thorough cleaning, an activity which can be very hazardous.

The potential for physical injury is obvious, and has been dealt with elsewhere. But the crucial threat of emotional trauma has long been ignored. This trauma is caused by the ignorance and inexperience of the stuffling and his owner. Prior to their first huggle, few stufflings have even heard of a bath or haircut, and find the experience terribly frightening.

> HAND WASH—GENTLE CYCLE.
> DO NOT IMMERSE! TOWEL DRY
> CONSIDERATELY. AVOID WRINGING,
> TWISTING, HANGING BY APPENDAGES.

Stuffed animals have fewer legal rights than a pair of shorts. They must be given the protection of bathing tags!

Improper handling put too much strain on this tail.

Both the emotional trauma and the physical danger must be eliminated if stuffies are to lead long, fearless lives. There are several possible ways of accomplishing this. They should be examined by every responsible owner.

Bathing

Legal protection holds the most promise of reducing the dangers of bathing. Stuffed animals have fewer legal rights than a pair of shorts. While most clothing has a tag with washing

instructions, stuffies have nothing at all. Owners are forced to choose between letting their stuffies remain soiled and guessing at the proper procedure. Disasters often result.

This cannot be allowed to continue. Stuffed animals must be given the protection of bathing tags! But this protection may take decades to establish, and something must be done in the meantime. The quickest solution is to teach owners a bathing procedure that avoids both psychic shock and physical injury.

Since even the gentlest method can be traumatic to a stuffling (see Glossary) undergoing his first bath, care must be taken to prepare him for the experience. This preparation involves the following steps:

1. Pick up and hug the stuffling. While holding him, tell him that you realize he does not enjoy being mussed or soiled, and that you are going to give him a bath to relieve his condition.

2. Describe the bath step by step, including moistening, soaping, rubbing, drying, and brushing.

3. Gather a huggle of older stuffies, each of whom has experienced at least one bath.

4. Place the stuffling in the huggle and leave. The older stuffies will reassure the stuffling.

5. While the stuffling is being reassured, prepare the bath. When it is ready, get the stuffling.

6. Bathe the stuffling with a moist

After the bath: toweling and reassurance.

towel or sponge. While bathing, describe each step (what you are going to do and why you are going to do it) to the stuffling.

7. All bathing must be done by hand. Machines like clothes washers are both physical and emotional hazards.

8. After the stuffling has been soaped and rinsed, rub with a towel. Use a hand-size blow dryer (on a mild setting—too much heat can damage delicate fur) to make sure he is completely dry.

Many inexperienced owners have never bathed a stuffie before and, despite the best directions, may stumble in the attempt. When a stuffie—even the most experienced—realizes that his owner is uncertain of the procedure, he will become nervous, and all reassurance will be useless. The only solution is practice, preferably on a stuffielike object.

There are a number of toys and clothing accessories that, while bearing a surface resemblance to stuffed animals, are completely lacking in any sense of self-awareness or personal identity. Objects like mufflers, bedroom slippers, stuffed balls, and earmuffs make excellent practice dummies since no one will be injured if a mistake is made.

Caution must also be exercised in the choice of bathing and grooming supplies. Although dogs, cats, horses, and many other animals all have specially designed bathing supplies,

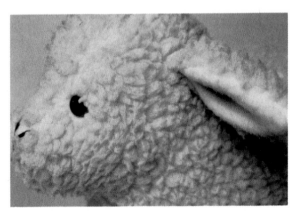

Brisk rubbing or careful blow drying adds the finishing touch to the bath.

stuffies do not. They have been completely ignored by the entire pet industry. Stuffies need special shampoos, brushes, clothes, combs, conditioners, and dryers. But none are available. This oversight means that owners must again pick and choose among numerous possible choices. Stuffies are sensitive to many chemicals and processes that do not affect other animals. Their shampoos, for instance, should be of the dry foam (low moisture content) type. Most human and animal shampoos need lots of water to work properly, and too much water can damage a stuffie. Unfortunately, few alternatives are available. So we suggest that only the mildest shampoos and rinses be used. Stuffies cannot regrow their fur easily, so be very careful with what they have.

Haircuts

While a new stuffling occasionally needs cosmetic adjustments, they should be made by experienced professionals only.

Unfortunately, the cosmetology industry has completely ignored this area. Fortunately, many cosmetology students practice on hairlike materials very similar to the fur on many stuffies. With additional experience on people or animals, many become fully qualified for work on stuffies. Some of these cosmetologists are stuffie owners themselves, and are very sympathetic to stuffie needs.

Dressing Up

Stuffed animals do not wear clothes to cover their "private parts." They don't have any to cover. But stuffies do wear clothes for protection, social occasions, and costume parties.

Stuffies are not bred for severe weather. They need protection from sun, wind, rain, snow, and other adverse conditions. Hats, coats, gloves, boots, sweaters, and other gear should always be worn when needed. Scarves are especially important for giraffes, and other stuffies find them flattering. Sunglasses and goggles must be carefully chosen or specially made. While nearly every monkey can be fitted successfully, few hedgehogs and virtually no snakes are able to wear readymade glasses.

Other articles of clothing that may cause problems are belts: most stuffies don't have waistlines! And mittens are usually preferred over long white kid gloves.

Many stuffies enjoy ballet, theater, and concerts, and most of them choose to dress for the occasion.

All stuffies enjoy costume parties. Some of the best are organized by STUFF (see Glossary). At these parties, people and stuffies mix, and share the latest news. New friendships are made, visits arranged, and prizes given. Everyone has a good time.

Stuffies are not bred for severe weather. Sunglasses and goggles afford protection from bright sun.

Of all stuffie activities, costume parties are the biggest favorite.

7. Training Your Stuffed Animal

Why to Train

Stuffies bred in large factories, stored in dull warehouses, and sold in crowded stores seldom see old stuffies or young children (their chief sources of wisdom), and must rely on their instincts for guidance. These instincts are of little help in choosing a spot, performing tricks, and behaving properly around people. Factory-bred stuffies need the knowledge and experience they have been denied.

While they will gain some of this knowledge in their first huggle, the necessary experience can be acquired only through a relationship with a human being. Since the key to this experience is the careful training undertaken by the stuffie and his owner, a training program is of vital importance to every stuffie's growth and development.

When to Start

The training program should begin at the first meeting. Any delay could allow a stuffling to develop habits that are impolite or dangerous. A good training program will provide the knowledge and experience the stuffie needs, and head off bad habits before they become established.

No stuffling wants to misbehave. But since their upbringing does not teach them to behave properly, they do make mistakes. Most young stufflings have never seen an electric appliance, fireplace, sink, toilet, oven, or

Left: A training program is of vital importance to every stuffie's growth and development.

any of the other strange and (to stufflings) fascinating objects that fill the average home. They wonder what they are, and if no one tells them, they will investigate for themselves. This is why the safety measures of chapter 5 are so necessary. Also, stufflings don't know anything about human social customs and physical limitations. They don't know that it is wrong to sleep on a dark stairway, tickle their sleeping owner's feet, or stare at a naked person. If patiently taught the ways of the world, and given access to older stuffies who already know them, they will rapidly perfect those habits that make stuffies so pleasant to have around.

The Training Mind

Stuffed animals are very sensitive to human attitudes. They respond to posture, voice, emotions, and thoughts. In training stuffies, this must be kept in mind. If the trainer's actions are disorganized, his voice cross, emotions aroused, or mind confused, then the stuffie will be unable to respond properly.

Two essential "seed ideas" can be used very effectively by the average owner:

1. "In order to train a stuffie you have to know more than the stuffie." This is neither as simple nor as obvious as it first appears. Many owners make the mistake of attempting to teach their stuffies to hold still. They're

An outing to a museum of art is an appropriate reward.

already much better at it than you are.

2. "While you are teaching a stuffie, the stuffie is teaching you." Stuffies teach by example. They constantly demonstrate how to be quiet, to listen, and to remain calm.

When properly understood, these seed ideas bring a closer understanding of stuffie needs and goals, and help the owner maximize his rapport with his stuffies.

The Lessons

Training stuffies requires the ability to distinguish between two types of tricks. There are skills that stuffies ex-

cel at, and there are tricks they are not equipped for. If an owner cannot tell the difference, his stuffies are in trouble. Fortunately, the category a trick belongs in is easily determined.

If it requires quick movements or strong muscles, a stuffie can't do it. They perform very poorly in sports like football, basketball, and soccer. And they particularly dislike being used as the ball! And attempts to teach them to fly by tossing them in the air will not be appreciated.

But if a trick requires patience, quiet, or self-control, they can do it. They are very good at sitting up, hiding, listening, telepathy, telekinesis,

Many owners make the mistake of attempting to teach their stuffies to sit still. They're already much better at it than you are.

The trainer encourages two
students in rolling over.

Right: Stuffies teach by example,
demonstrating how to be quiet,
to listen, and to remain calm.

and many other sedentary activities.

Stuffed animals are very intelligent, and learn quickly when the correct method is used. The following method has been tested with numerous stuffies of varying backgrounds, and has proved effective in most cases:

1. Describe the trick or rule. Be sure to present it as a game (if a trick) or as serious (if a rule).

2. While describing the trick, visualize or imagine the stuffie performing it. A "mental image" will help the stuffie "see" what the trainer wants him to do.

3. Demonstrate the trick by acting it out. The trainer will sit up, play dead, roll over, etc.

4. Help the stuffie assume the pose required for the trick.

5. Congratulate the stuffie. A hug is always a good reward, but some stuffies need an additional prize (such

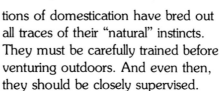
as an outing to a museum of art) to reinforce their behavior. The stuffie himself will let you know the appropriate treat.

This is the standard method of teaching physical tricks and skills. It is similar to methods used with other animals.

Field Training

Stuffed animals are virtually helpless in the wild. Thousands of generations of domestication have bred out all traces of their "natural" instincts. They must be carefully trained before venturing outdoors. And even then, they should be closely supervised.

Field training includes preparatory measures and survival techniques. The survival techniques are fairly simple and easily taught. They include:

1. Hiding: Stuffies are very good at this, but need help finding and getting to a good spot. This spot can be

Stuffed animals are very intelligent and learn
quickly when the correct method is used.

in a tree, on a fence, under a bush,
behind a rock, or anyplace else that
hides them from predators and pro-
tects them from weather.

2. Holding Still: Stuffies are better at this than any other animal, but
should be reminded to remain ab-
solutely motionless when outdoors.

3. Keeping Quiet: Stuffies have
been known to go for weeks without
making a sound. But lack of noise is
not enough for safety. Animals are
very sensitive to emotions, so complete silence, including thoughts and
feelings as well as sounds, is needed.

4. Invisibility: Total mastery of
the preceding skills can lead to this
ability. If a stuffie is becoming this
good, be careful to remember where
he is.

The preparatory measures must
be utilized each and every time a stuffie ventures outdoors. Specifics vary
from one place to another, but the
following cover most conditions:

1. Check the weather. Stuffies
have little resistance to rain, snow,
hail, wind, or sunshine. If any of these
conditions exists, then stuffies should
be dressed accordingly.

2. Watch out for cats, dogs, and
other predators. Stuffies are very poor
runners, and will need to be rescued if
mistaken for prey.

3. Never leave stuffies out in the
open. When they're easily seen, the
best hiding skills are useless.

4. Don't leave them outdoors
alone! If you are not *right there* when

Stuffies love to dress up, but they should be appropriately attired whether for sun or snow.

Not all stuffies are perfect, but disciplining can be difficult.
They don't eat dinner, so it can't be taken away from them.

wind, rain, a predator, or whatever comes along, the stuffie will be helpless.

The one essential element of field trips is safety. Field training and preparatory measures were designed for this purpose, and should be used every time a stuffie ventures outdoors. Failure to do so could result in tragedy.

How Your Stuffie Teaches You

The biggest impediment to improved treatment of stuffed animals is owner illiteracy. A stuffie doesn't have a chance, unless he can get his message across to his owner.

Most owners are most receptive during those periods of sleep when their brain is at rest. Their thoughts, feelings, desires, and the interference they cause are at their lowest, and some of the stuffie's message can get through then. Working on this principle, stuffies have developed a very effective Sleep-Teaching technique. It does, however, have a serious flaw: the very condition that makes it possible. The unconscious owner is unable to interpret or respond to the stuffie's lessons. They have to be kept simple and repetitive if they are to have any impact, but the effect is very calming.

Many owners discover that the calming effect is increased with proximity, and soon learn to sleep with their stuffies. The stuffie messages relieve the owner's tensions, help him relax, and relieve the stuffie's need to be needed.

If you are not *right there* when wind or whatever comes along, the stuffie will be helpless.

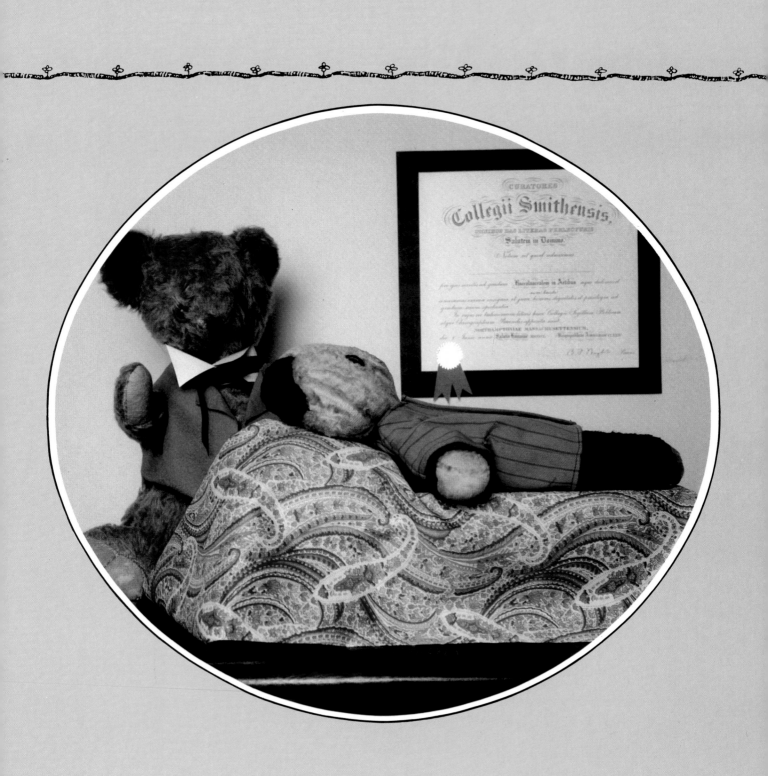

Stuffies do not have vital organs, bones, or blood, so they cannot injure, break, or lose any. Stuffed animals do not get colds, fevers, chills or coughs. But they do get sick. Although they are immune to germs, viruses, allergies, and parasites, they often suffer from mental, emotional, and nervous disorders. While these are usually no more serious than a common cold, they can become dangerous if ignored.

Even professionals find understanding these illnesses difficult. The rarity of stuffiologists and their medical specialists, the absence of funds, and the refusal of scientific journals to publish their research, have made the accumulation of facts very slow.

Owners have been left without any means of diagnosis or treatment for much too long. A special study was undertaken by the Stuffie Medical Research Center (SMERC) to provide this desperately needed information. The results are here made public for the first time. It is hoped that this information will encourage better care of stuffed animals, and stimulate interest in further research.

Mental Illness

The most common mental illness is "self-denial." Like other mental illnesses, it begins as a negative idea accidentally impressed on the stuffie by a human being. No human is perfect. It is a fact of life that all owners occasionally have a negative

8. Health and First Aid

Be careful not to express negative thoughts around stuffies. They are extremely impressionable.

Left: Stuffed animals do not get colds, but they often suffer from mental, emotional, and nervous disorders.

There has been some success with the introduction of self-affirming ideas.

thought or emotion. As long as this is mild, no harm is done. But when it becomes severe, it can present quite a problem.

Self-denial begins when a stuffling accepts the idea that stuffed animals are lifeless, inanimate toys. When the owner begins to believe this, his stuffies are in trouble. Stuffies are very trusting creatures, especially of those closest to them. They are very receptive to anything their owner says, feels, or thinks about them. When an owner strongly disbelieves in his stuffies' existence, they believe him!

The stuffie soon stops thinking, feeling, and moving. An owner observing a stuffie in this condition will be unable to perceive any sign of life. It is buried too deeply to see. This further reinforces the owner's negative thoughts and their effects, and creates a vicious cycle leading to complete oblivion for the stuffie.

When self-denial has advanced this far, it is extremely difficult to cure. There has been some success with the purposeful introduction of self-affirming ideas. But this is a complex experimental procedure and should not be attempted by untrained owners.

The best treatments currently available are prevention and time. Placing the stuffie in a foster home, sending him to visit a friend, or giving him to a new owner can prevent self-denial and similar illnesses.

When it is too late to prevent the illness, then the stuffies must be given time. They can heal themselves if placed in a positive environment. A little peace, quiet, and a good huggle go a long way.

Emotional Illness

Stuffed animals are susceptible to two different types of emotional disease: empathic illness and emotional trauma. The chief difference between the two is their source of origin.

Empathic illness originates in the relationship between a stuffie and his

Stuffies can heal themselves if placed in a positive environment.

owner. During adjustment and acceptance, a stuffie is very sensitive to the emotional activity of his owner, but is too immature to protect himself from negative emotions. When his owner is angry, depressed, frustrated, or confused, he is angry, depressed, frustrated, or confused also. Since a stuffie's health depends on his ability to give and receive love, these negative emotions have a severely debilitating effect. And if they continue, they can result in permanent damage.

Stuffiologists specializing in empathic illness are called empathologists. A very dedicated group, they are severely overworked and underfinanced. If there were more of them, more could be done. But under the present handicaps, they have yet to find a means to cure or prevent this type of disease.

Meanwhile, empirical research has indicated that the best home remedy for empathic illness is to form a huggle with the ill owner and all his stuffies. Encourage the owner to cuddle, hug, and otherwise demonstrate his affection for his stuffies.

Not only does this technique reassure the stuffie, it also calms the owner. (Who can stay upset while cuddling a stuffie?) When the owner relaxes, both he and his stuffie are well on the way to recovery.

Fortunately, most cases prove to be of this mild, temporary nature, and healthy stuffies quickly recover from occasional bouts. But when the owner makes a habit of throwing emotional fits, the effects last longer. A permanent solution must then be found.

Emotional trauma is an emotional disturbance that originates within the stuffie. Although it is less common than empathic illness, its effects can be just as debilitating. A common form is frequently contracted by stuffies sold at garage and yard sales. Being cast off like an object of little worth or value would damage anyone's ego. When this is done to a stuffie by the one person he has trusted and depended on, the results can be tragic.

There are many alternatives open to the owner who loses interest in one or more stuffies. He can give them away, put them in hibernation, or see a psychiatrist. But he should not sell them. It destroys the confidence, joy, and creativity of the abandoned stuffies, and undermines the trust of the remaining pets.

Nervous Disease

A major impediment to treating both mental and emotional illnesses is the inability of even highly trained professionals to discern their presence. Fortunately, another kind of diagnosis is available to the owner. Both kinds of illness produce physical symptoms that are easily identified.

Stuffies are very orderly animals with regular habits. A sudden change in these habits can indicate both the

presence and type of disease. A wanderer who gradually stops wandering may be mentally ill. The idea that he is not real brings a slow halt to all activity.

In contrast, an emotional illness strikes suddenly and has an immediate effect. An emotionally distracted stuffie will find himself falling—sometimes into a dangerous spot.

Thus a nervous disease, while a danger in itself, can also be a warning. It provides definite physical evidence that something is wrong. The watch-

The best remedy for empathic illnesses is to form a huggle.

The first rule of First Aid is: Stay Calm! Avoid owner panic.

ful owner is provided with the clues
he needs to diagnose and treat his
stuffies.

First Aid

1. The first rule of First Aid is:
Stay Calm! The biggest danger of a
medical emergency is owner panic.
Breathe slowly and deeply, relax tense
muscles, and comfort your stuffie.

When these preliminaries are
complete, you can go on to the next
procedure, *but not before!*

2. Examine the stuffie to determine the extent and cause of the injury (wear, mishandling, mental or
emotional illness, etc.). Discuss your
diagnosis with your wise old stuffies.
Outline a therapy program (including mental, emotional, and physical
therapies, as needed). *And don't let
it happen again!*

3. If you decide that the injury
is beyond your abilities, then send a
description of the type and extent of
the injuries/illness to SMERC (see
Glossary) care of STUFF (see Glossary). The staff is well versed in stuffie
medical needs and keeps a list of hos-
pital facilities open to stuffed animals.
And members of STUFF can call the
local Emergency Hotline established
for their use.

4. *Above all:* Be careful, follow
the handling instructions, and cud-
dle/hug your stuffies frequently. These
are the best guarantees that you'll
never need this chapter.

Stuffed animals are virtually
helpless in the wild.

9. Breeding and Reproduction

While the mechanics of stuffie reproduction are well known, the activity that precedes and stimulates the mechanics has remained a mystery. Stuffies obviously cannot reproduce in the usual manner. They lack the necessary equipment. But this lack has never hampered their efforts. They have done so well with their own method that they are experiencing an unprecedented population explosion.

The unfortunate neglect of stuffies by the scientific community delayed discovery of this method for many years. It was unearthed by SMERC only after exhaustive investigation, interviews, and analysis. The investigators found the results astounding. The method used, its relation to stuffie-owner interdependence, and its revelation of stuffie gender went far beyond anything they had imagined.

Male and Female Stuffies

One of the first duties of a new owner is to give his stuffling a carefully chosen name. Names perform several functions. They identify a stuffie as a person with an identity of his own. They describe various aspects of that identity. And they indicate the stuffie's gender. But since stuffies don't have the physical equipment that distinguishes male/female, how can they be either one?

The answer lies in their personality. Human psychology has identified several mental and emotional patterns

Left: Stuffies obviously cannot reproduce in the usual manner. They lack the necessary equipment.

. . . But this lack has never hampered their efforts.

or tendencies that differentiate male and female. Stuffie psychology has found this to be equally true of stuffed animals. A male stuffie is different from a female stuffie because of his psychological makeup. Shoppers sense this difference and choose a stuffling of the appropriate gender. When naming a stuffling, the owner unconsciously takes the stuffie's gender into consideration.

Research into the precise nature, effects, and functions of these gender differences has only begun, and is far from complete. So, little more can be said on the subject at this time.

How Stuffies Do It

It has long been known that the relationship between stuffies and owners is a mutually beneficial one—what is technically known as symbiotic. But the precise contributions and activities of stuffies have long remained hidden and been little understood. This includes their gift of affection, their demonstration of love,

and their breeding practices.

These breeding practices were the most difficult to uncover. The best evidence currently available indicates that since they do not have the ability to reproduce themselves, they borrow the abilities of their owners, and through their owners the resources and skills of humanity. A network of stuffies, owners, and breeders enables stuffed animals to stimulate stuffie reproduction and influence their own evolution. This networking has contributed to their unprecedented popularity, a skyrocketing population, and an astounding diversity of breeds. Unusual though it is, their method is an unqualified success.

Above: Although their breeding practices remain a mystery, stuffies have evolved an astounding diversity of breeds.

Left: Networking has contributed to a skyrocketing population.

10. Photographing Stuffed Animals

Photographing stuffies is a delightful pastime that can easily become a favorite hobby. The legendary patience of stuffed animals make stuffies a photographer's dream. A stuffie never breaks a pose and can hold a smile indefinitely. A photographer can take as long as he needs posing the stuffie and adjusting his equipment. Photos can be taken in dim light without fear that the stuffie will move and blur. And they greet every picture with the same fresh smile.

Stuffies should be carefully groomed before a photo session. They always like to look their best, especially when their appearance is being recorded.

Backgrounds can be very important, especially in a portrait. Be careful to choose a setting that shows the stuffies' best features.

While most stuffies enjoy the attention of being photographed, it is an unusual experience, which can be frightening. They should be prepared beforehand by the following method:

1. Be sure the stuffies know the photographer. Stuffed animals tend to be less certain of themselves around strangers. Simply introduce everyone and make sure that everyone is relaxed and friendly.

2. Show the stuffies the camera, and a photograph of yourself, and explain what the camera does and what the photo is for. They will settle down and give you their best smile.

3. Stuffed animals will not move

Left: The legendary patience of stuffed animals makes them a photographer's dream.

Right: Stuffed animals greet every picture with the same fresh smile.

Stuffies should be carefully groomed before a photo session.

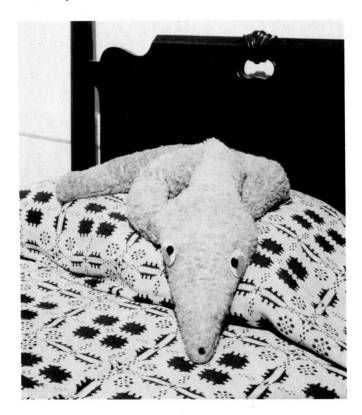

or levitate in the presence of a camera, so you will have to pose them. Be gentle, and explain what you are doing.

4. Take your time. The stuffies aren't going anywhere.

Individuals

Stuffed animals are photographed to record special events like outings, visits, or parties, to provide a picture to show friends, to advertise or sell a particular breed, or to enter a STUFF show or contest. While the photographer is capturing and manipulating the visual image, the stuffie is creating and impressing the emotional image.

Stuffed animals put a little of their love into each photograph. This gives the photos some of the vitality and effect of a real stuffie. Since stuffies alter their effects to match the need at hand, they should be told the purpose of the current photograph, and given a moment to adjust their effect accordingly.

Huggles

Every experienced photographer knows how difficult it is to get a large group to pose for a camera. Someone is always blinking, sneezing, coughing, talking, moving, making faces, or something! But with stuffies this is not a problem. They just sit there, patiently holding their pose and waiting for the photographer to finish.

Unfortunately, excessive cooperation of this type can be dangerous. Portrait photography requires diplomacy, experience, and patience. Stuffies are so cooperative that very little patience is needed. A photographer who grows accustomed to stuffies may lose his patience, and be unable to work with less cooperative subjects. This danger can be avoided by continuing to photograph demanding subjects that force you to exercise your self-control.

Fortunately, stuffies do need some help preparing for a group photograph. Here are several steps that should not be ignored:

1. Huggles are traditionally posed in a manner reflecting the family relationships.When the owner is present, he is usually seated in the center of the picture with his oldest stuffie in his lap and his other stuffies gathered about him. When the owner is not in the photo (as when he is holding the camera), the older stuffies are traditionally placed in the center.

2. New stufflings should not be placed *on the edge* of the picture. This can make them feel isolated and unwanted. Place them near the center, where they can receive the encouragement and attention they need.

3. All the stuffies should be visible. If they cannot be seen, they will not be able to make an *effective* impression on the photograph. Facial features are especially important since they transmit much of the impression.

4. Make allowances for differences in size and color. Small light-colored stuffies should be in front, and large dark stuffies in the rear.

5. Be creative. Stuffies like to experiment.

6. While most stuffies have little knowledge of or experience with photography, they do have an excellent sense of proportion and propriety. So be sure to ask them for ideas. They may have some excellent suggestions.

Indoors

Stuffed animals have always spent most of their time indoors. This places them in close contact with human beings and creates a multitude of photographic opportunities. These include parties, visits, crises, shows, holidays, and daily activities of all sorts.

The type of photograph taken and the feeling the stuffie gives it are largely determined by the nature of the event being recorded. Owners have a tendency to fall into a repetitive rut. Photographing daily activities can give new meaning and direction to familiar events, and stimulate new projects. Photos of these activities should examine the changing detail that keeps them new and fascinating.

However, crises, dangers, and accidents are rare events that should not be repeated. Having a photograph of them reminds stuffies and owners

A photographer can take as long as he needs. The stuffies aren't going anywhere.

Outdoor activities—including smelling flowers—should be recorded when possible.

of the circumstances that created them, and indicates means of preventing their reoccurrence. Photos of these events should emphasize dark threatening colors, and capture the danger or tragedy of the situation.

Parties, visits, and shows are festive affairs with games, contests, discussion, and gossip. Photos of these events should emphasize bright

cheerful colors and capture the stuffies' joyful and exuberant behavior.

Outdoors

Stuffies usually venture outdoors only on special occasions like picnics, hikes, and field trials. Since these are special events, many owners record the occasion on film. Photographing stuffies can be a delightful addition to the day's activities. But the owner must be careful not to allow it to distract him from the need for preparatory measures and survival techniques. Many stuffies have been endangered when their owner became so involved with capturing the photograph that he forgot to watch for dangerous situations.

With this caution in mind, there are a variety of reasons for and advantages to photographing stuffies outdoors.

Outdoor photos can be an excellent study aid for survival training and field trials. Just as athletes use television to study and improve their technique, stuffies can use still photography to improve hiding, holding still, remaining quiet, invisibility, and other outdoor skills.

The skills used in field trials and other outdoor events take time and practice to develop. Photographs are an essential part of the practice sessions. They give both stuffie and owner a permanent record of past achievements, and indicate areas that need improvement.

Photographs of stuffies are records of happy times with good friends.

Picnics and hikes offer many opportunities to observe stuffies in activities that are difficult or impossible indoors. These activities include smelling flowers, climbing trees, and talking with elves, and should be recorded when possible.

Photographs of stuffies are records of happy times with good friends, and help preserve many fond memories.

11. Parties and Shows

Stuffie parties and shows are unique events embodying a spirited exchange of joy, wonder, and fellowship. Stuffies and owners meet, socialize, make friends, play games, arrange visits, plan hunts, and hold STUFF (see Glossary) contests and meetings. Stuffie parties were once rare, disorganized affairs, but with the organization of STUFF this changed. The national network of "Chapters" and "Regions" now holds organized events at regular intervals. While almost anyone can hold a stuffie party, the official STUFF events provide variety and fellowship unavailable anywhere else.

Parties

While stuffed animals turn otherwise average parties into extraordinary events, their limitations must be kept in mind. There are many things that they cannot do, and there are several that should not be done to them. Because of this, stuffie birthdays (day of first adoption), commemorative holidays, seasonal holidays, and other events are celebrated somewhat uniquely. A stuffie is not expected to blow out the candles on his cake. Nor is it usual for him to eat it. And when playing a board game, he does have trouble moving the pieces. Stuffies can take part in these activities, but only with their owner's help. Fortunately, helping the stuffies is half the fun!

Unfortunately, many substances

Human judges have a difficult time measuring stuffie skills like remaining quiet, listening, and hiding.

Left: Stuffie parties and shows are unique events embodying spirited exchanges of joy, wonder, and fellowship.

Stuffed animals turn otherwise average parties into extraordinary events.

commonly found at parties should not be used around stuffies. This includes cigarettes, alcohol, and other drugs. These substances are dangerous to stuffies and inhibit stuffie-owner rapport. So their use is discouraged.

STUFF Shows

At most animal shows, the judges measure physical skills and breed quality. But at stuffie shows, this isn't possible. Human judges have a very difficult time measuring a stuffie's ability to perform basic tricks like sitting or holding still. We just do not have the patience to watch and wait for several months. And other stuffie skills like remaining quiet, listening, and hiding pose similar difficulties.

Breed quality meets much the same problem. Stuffies don't have genes or bloodlines, so there is no such thing as a purebred stuffie. While there have been attempts to classify stuffies by size, shape, age, or conformity to some vague human ideal, these qualities have little relationship to the stuffie's true nature.

Types of Shows

There are many types of STUFF shows, but most fall in one of five categories:
1. Costume Parties
2. Safety Training
3. Field Trials
4. Personal Experience
5. Hunts

Most are open to all STUFF members regardless of age, breed, and previous experience. Each category has its own appeal, and many stuffies develop a favorite.

Costume Parties are the biggest favorite. They frequently have a theme, but are often freestyle. All costumes must be made by the owner or an immediate family member. And the stuffie must have been in the owner's huggle for at least six weeks.

Safety Training is a test of the stuffie's skill and the owner's knowledge. Stuffies tour a carefully designed course (with their owners) and try to spot hazardous situations. The tour is timed, and the stuffie's ability to spot and correct the dangers is graded.

Field Trials are a test of stuffie survival techniques under actual and simulated conditions. Outdoor skills like hiding, holding still, and remaining quiet are demonstrated and judged.

Personal Experience is a written description of unusual events that color the stuffies' lives. Short stories describing these events are written by the owners and submitted to the *Stuffed News Journal*. The winners may receive a cash prize and have their stories published.

Hunts are organized shopping trips. The Hunters (shoppers) gather before the trip, and each describes as best he can the type of stuffie he is

The birthday party, even without cake and candles, is a high point in a stuffie's year.

hunting for. The hunters share likely and possible locations where various stuffies may be found, and divide into groups of two, three, or four hunters. Each group then goes in search of their stuffies. When they return from their quest (at a specified time), each hunter describes his experience and introduces his new stuffling.

As the number of entries grows, the shows can become too large for the intimate groups that stuffies prefer. In order to keep them small, large groups are divided into smaller groups or classes. The most popular is the "Bred-by-Exhibitor" class. It is open to all stuffies bred by their owner or his immediate family. Most classes can be used in conjunction with any category. but the "Bred-by-Exhibitor" class is one of the few that can also be used as a category.

Other classes include the "Stuffling" class, which is open to all the stuffies aged twelve months or less; the "Senior Stuffie" class, which is

open to all stuffies aged ten years or more; and the "Novice" class, which is open to all stuffies aged six months or more who have never won a first prize in any show.

In addition to Chapter and Regional events, at least one National Show is held every year. The category of the Show is chosen by the members and varies from year to year.

How to Enter

All stuffed animals registered with STUFF can enter any show for which they qualify. Forthcoming shows are listed in the *Stuffed News Journal* and announced in Chapter newsletters. When you find a show you are interested in, simply write or call the Chapter or Regional Secretary (whichever is appropriate) and ask to be sent an entry packet. When you receive the packet, fill out the entry form and return it with the required fee. This fee is usually no more than a few dollars, but it can also take the form of a dish of food when the occasion includes a potluck dinner.

Nonmembers are welcome to join STUFF at any time. All stuffed animals are considered honorary members, but their owners have to sign up, pay dues, and be accompanied by a stuffie at all events. Information on where and how to apply can be obtained by writing or calling the local branch of the Stuffed Toys' Union.

Safety training: Stuffies tour a carefully designed course and try to spot hazardous situations.

12. The Aged Stuffed Animal

While stuffed animals have the longest lifespan of any known animal, very few of them live for more than a few decades. Most stuffies fall prey to owner ignorance while relatively young, and don't have time to gain the wisdom and experience of a mature stuffie. Their lives are too short.

This fate is completely foreign to natural stuffie experience, and should be corrected, While stuffiologists are still searching for the necessary treatment, it is obvious that the only permanent solution lies in overcoming owner ignorance. Only when owners treat their pets with love and affection will stuffies live long healthy happy lives.

Owner Ignorance

No one can survive when denied the care and attention he needs. This is as true of stuffies as it is of dogs, cats, horses, or any other animal. Unfortunately, stuffie needs are very difficult to detect. Countless generations of owners have been unable to give their stuffed animals the care and attention they needed. The owners simply didn't know how!

Stuffiologists believe that owner ignorance was the major cause of the near extinction of stuffies during the Intermediate period. While modern owners have had much more success than their predecessors, this is largely due to improved stuffie skills and not to owner knowledge. Modern owners

Left: Old stuffies never die.

are still woefully uninformed, and frequently make mistakes.

When denied proper care, stuffies wear quickly and soon look disheveled, threadbare, and old. When denied affection, they're much more sensitive to empathic illness, emotional trauma, and other debilitating diseases. If denied both, they age very quickly and must soon abandon their bodies. Thus owner ignorance is the primary cause of premature aging in stuffies.

Owners who give their stuffies lots of love, affection, and care find that their stuffies experience little wear or disease and remain healthy and happy for a very long time.

The Sad Event

All good stuffies must come to an end. Even with the best care, the day comes when the old stuffie must pass beyond the veil of life. Few owners understand the need for this event, and many seek to delay or prevent it. All life is born, matures, ages, and dies. To attempt to deny a stuffie the full experience is to deny him his next step. Sad as it makes us feel, the day comes when we must relinquish our hold on our stuffies and let them pass on.

When this occurs, the owner is faced with a dilemma. How do you dispose of a deceased stuffie? All societies have traditions and customs that guide the disposal of human and animal remains. But the traditions sur-

In the golden years, exciting outings give way to quiet pursuits.

Stuffed animals have the longest lifespan of any known animal.

rounding stuffie burial were lost during the Intermediate period. The surviving physical evidence indicates that Totemic owners interred their stuffies in stone crypts. But interment or burial may not be a proper disposal method for stuffies bred from nondegradable materials. Cremation could be used, but many of the modern materials give off dangerous gases when burned. Other methods are being considered, but all have similar difficulties. We suggest asking your stuffie or (if no longer possible) consulting with his friends about your stuffie's preference.

The remains of flowers, food,

and personal artifacts in early crypts indicate that Totemic interment was accompanied by considerable ceremony. While the original ceremony is long forgotten, the Stuffed Toys' Union has designed several modern versions. The shortest is quite simple:

Just give your stuffie one last hug.

Where Stuffies Go

The question of where stuffies go when they die is a major source of dispute among stuffiologists. Most have difficulty remaining properly objective about an afterlife, and would like to rely on their own beliefs or stuffie comments. But like any other science, stuffiology must rely on observation, not personal opinion. Since the problem is difficult to observe, and almost impossible to verify, it must remain unanswered for now.

But that doesn't prevent stuffiologists from discussing it. Fortunately, we tend to giggle, chuckle, and laugh while discussing the technical minutiae of our field. Giggles are incompatible with shouting matches, so the debate remains friendly. Currently two viewpoints seem dominant. Some believe that "where stuffies go" is a theological question, and has no place in a serious science like stuffiology. Others maintain that stuffiology isn't exactly a "serious" science, and can examine any question pertaining to stuffed animals. But all agree on one point:

Old stuffies never die, they just wear away.

Owner ignorance is the primary cause of premature aging in stuffies.

Almost invariably friendly, stuffed animals seldom if ever bite.

Glossary

abandonment (ə ban' dən mənt). *n.* 1. desertion of a stuffed animal. 2. throwing out of a stuffie.

acceptance (ak sep' təns). *n.* the mature stage of the relationship between a stuffie and his friend.

adoption (ə dop' shən). *n.* the process by which a human person acquires a stuffed animal for a companion.

breed (brēd). *n.* any homogeneous group of stuffed animals.

breed (brēd). *v.* to design and manufacture the bodies of stuffed animals.

breeder (brēd' ər). *n.* one who designs or manufactures the bodies of stuffed animals.

empathic illness (em pa' thik il' nəs). *n.* the effect of anger or other emotional outbursts on stuffies, especially when expressed by owner.

empathology (em' pə thol' ə jē). *n.* the science that studies the effects of human emotional outbursts on stuffed animals.

flopsy (flop' sē). *n.* an illness resulting from the degradation or loss of stuffing.

huggle (hug' əl). *n.* 1. a gathering of stuffies. 2. = hug: a therapeutic practice used to comfort young, sick, or disturbed stuffed animals. 3. a group hug.

invisibility (in viz' ə bil' ə tē). *n.* the stuffies' ability to make their presence imperceptible.

mange (mānj). *n.* hair loss due to poor anchorage of fur; generally caused by breeder negligence. *Obsolete.*

nervous disease (nər' vəs də' zēz). *n.* disruption of the stuffie nervous system usually caused by mental or emotional illness.

recognition (rek' əg nish' ən). *n.* the realization, by both stuffed animal and shopper, that each possesses those qualities for which each had been looking.

S.A. (es ā). *n.* abbreviation of "stuffed animal."

seam rip (sēm rip). *n.* failure of seams due to wear, mishandling, weak material, or poor stitching.

SMERC (smərk). *n.* acronym for the Stuffie Medical Research Center, the research arm of the Stuffed Toys' Union.

SNJ (es en jā). *n.* acronym for the *Stuffed News Journal*, the newsletter of the Stuffed Toys' Union.

spot (spot). *n.* a stuffed animal's favorite or preferred place.

STUFF (stuf). *n.* acronym for the Stuffed Toys' Union and the Friends of the Furred, an organization of stuffies and owners that holds shows, gives parties, and seeks to establish legal rights for stuffed animals.

stufficide (stuf' ə sīd). *n.* the killing of a stuffed animal, whether through intent or neglect.

stuffie (stuf' ē). *n.* 1. an adult stuffed animal. 2. any stuffed animal.

stuffiology (stuf' ē ol' ə jē). *n.* the science that deals with the origin, customs, history, etc., of stuffed animals.

stuffling (stuf' ling). *n.* a baby or child stuffie.

Totemic (tō tem' ik). *n.* earliest known period of stuffie development; concurrent with human Paleolithic period.

wanderer (wän' dər ər). *n.* any stuffed animal that habitually roams about.

Acknowledgments

No project of this scope can or should be the work of any one person. More people, groups, and stuffies have helped shape it than can be recognized. But I would like to thank D. K., H. B., Bumper, the Group, Georgia, Sarah, my Mom and Dad, Tracy, Ryan, Kathy K., Tina, Dennis, Miss Wulff; the staffs of: the Stuffed Toys' Union, the Stuffie Medical Research Center, the *Stuffed News Journal;* the Whittier, La Mirada, Fullerton, and Norwalk public libraries; the Cal-State Fullerton and Cal-State Long Beach libraries; Phyllis, Jeanne, Darilyn, and all the Abramsites; and my own wonderful stuffies: Dog, Buddy, Whoppo, Wumpus, Perfessor, Owl, C. P., Sam, Barney, Bill, Albert, Spike, Cindy, Caterpiggle, Rufus, Max, Wacko Jack, and all of the stuffies and people who made this book possible.

G. K.

Special Thanks

The publishers are very grateful to the store owners, distributors, manufacturers, and friends who let us keep their stuffies overnight, and sometimes longer, for photography:

Alresford, Anima, Avanti, Eden, Gund, The Penny Whistle, Ramat, Reeves International, Inc., Sakai & Co., F.A.O. Schwarz (especially Mr. De Fini), Steiff, Trupa, Wallace Berrie & Company, Inc.; countless friends and neighbors.

It was wrenching, after working with the stuffies and getting to know them, to give them all back.

We also wish to thank those people—particularly the Warner family—who let us barge in, push their furniture around, and take pictures in their apartments; and Mary Hilliard for her excellent help on some of the styling.